VIDEO GAME DESIGNER

KEVIN CUNNINGHAM

Published in the United States of America by Cherry Lake Publishing
Ann Arbor, Michigan
www.cherrylakepublishing.com

Content Adviser: Dr. Scott M. Martin, founding director, Computer Game Design Program, Virginia Serious Game
Institute (VSGI), George Mason University, Fairfax, Virginia
Reading Adviser: Marla Conn, ReadAbility, Inc.

Photo Credits: ©Dejan Stanic Micko/Shutterstock Images, cover, 1 ; © JUAN CARLOS ROJAS/NOTIMEX/Newscom, 5;
© Stefano Tinti/Shutterstock.com, 6, 7, 27; © Dikiiy/Shutterstock.com, 11; © zeljkodan/Shutterstock Images, 12;
© Geber86/iStockphoto, 14; © Monkey Business Images, 17, 23; © Vancouver Film School/http://www.flickr.com/, 18;
© diversepixel/Shutterstock Images, 19; © DM7/Shutterstock Images, 20; © DragonImages/Thinkstock, 24; CC-BY-2.0,
© RubberBall/Alamy, 28

Library of Congress Cataloging-in-Publication Data

Cunningham, Kevin, 1966- author.
  Video game designer/Kevin Cunningham.
    pages cm.—(Cool STEAM careers)
  Summary: "Readers will learn what it takes to succeed as a video game designer. The book also explains the necessary
educational steps, useful character traits, potential hazards, and daily job tasks related to this career. Sidebars include
thought-provoking trivia. Questions in the backmatter ask for text-dependent analysis. Photos, a glossary, and additional
resources are included."—Provided by publisher.
  Audience: Ages 8–12
  Audience: Grades 4 to 6
  Includes bibliographical references and index.
  ISBN 978-1-63362-567-9 (hardcover)—ISBN 978-1-63362-657-7 (pbk.)—ISBN 978-1-63362-747-5 (pdf)—
ISBN 978-1-63362-837-3 (ebook)
  1. Video games—Design—Vocational guidance—Juvenile literature. 2. Video games industry—Vocational guidance
Juvenile literature. 3. Computer games—Programming—Vocational guidance—Juvenile literature. I. Title. II. Series:
21st century skills library. Cool STEAM careers.

  QA76.76.C672C86 2016
  794.8'1536—dc23
                        2015005367

Cherry Lake Publishing would like to acknowledge the work of
the Partnership for 21st Century Skills. Please visit www.p21.org
for more information.

ABOUT THE AUTHOR

Kevin Cunningham is the author of 60 books, including a series on diseases in history and books
in Cherry Lake's Global Products series. He lives near Chicago, Illinois.

TABLE OF CONTENTS

STEAM is the acronym for Science, Technology, Engineering, Arts, and Mathematics. In this book, you will read about how each of these study areas is connected to a career in video game design.

CHAPTER 1

THE EVOLUTION OF VIDEO GAMES

Rob leaned into the office. He looked worried. "Anna," he said, "we have an issue."

"Another one?" Anna asked.

"A collision bug sends Captain Hero crashing through the deck of the ghost ship. Why do these **glitches** keep happening?"

Anna closed her laptop and reached for the phone. "Have no fear. I'll get the programmers working on the collision bug right away."

Anna designs video games. She loves her job.

It allows her to turn her creativity loose to create fantastic games played by millions of people. Even stressful days are great. After all, being a video game designer means solving problems. It also means long hours and dealing with tough deadlines. But Anna feels lucky to have such a unique and exciting career.

Shigeru Miyamoto of Nintendo is one of the world's top video game designers.

Nolan Bushnell started the Atari Corporation in the 1970s. The company sold 20 million units of the Atari 2600.

The first video games hit stores in 1972. Four years earlier, engineer Ralph H. Baer had designed the Magnavox Odyssey, also known as the Brown Box. Baer designed the Odyssey to play video games on a television. The Brown Box soon became a must-have gift at birthdays and holiday time.

Video game fan Nolan Bushnell and engineer Al Alcorn took the idea further. They built on the Odyssey's table tennis game and created *Pong*. Once Bushnell put

Pong on his Atari home console, it became the first home video game hit.

In the late 1970s and early 1980s, gamers went to **arcades**. They dropped their quarters into popular games like *Pac-Man, Space Invaders,* and *Donkey Kong.* The last, created by Nintendo Games mastermind Shigeru Miyamoto, costarred a hero named Mario.

By playing video games as kids, many designers found their passions early.

In recent years, video game graphics have improved.

Soon, Mario and his brother, Luigi, jumped to their own game, *Super Mario Bros.* It launched the most successful video game **franchise** of all time.

Engineers and programmers teamed up to make gaming consoles and computers able to do more. As sound effects and graphics improved, huge numbers of people joined the gaming world.

Sports games, such as *Madden NFL*, put players in the middle of National Football League action. Role-playing games (RPGs) like the *Final Fantasy* series brought cutting-edge graphics and heart-pounding game play.

Companies had to hire whole teams of programmers, artists, and others to pull off these complex games. Designers, meanwhile, shifted to providing ideas and leadership.

Entertainment companies invested millions in their gaming divisions. The industry boomed. In 2013, video game sales topped $20.5 billion. New games in big-name franchises like *Halo* and *Destiny* often made more money than successful movies.

The video game industry continues to grow. More than ever, companies need designers with the talents and skills to create the great games of the future.

THINK ABOUT TECHNOLOGY

The word augmented means "added to" or "made bigger." Many experts believe augmented reality games will be the next big thing. In an augmented reality game, players step away from the TV or computer. They use a smartphone or a wearable computer to see the local park as an alien planet or their neighborhood as a town made from LEGOs. Players move around on missions or use a game controller to change their augmented surroundings.

CHAPTER 2

ON THE JOB

A video game designer learns the job one way: through experience. He or she starts his or her career as a member of a design team. There, the person works on helping a lead designer turn ideas into a product for eager players.

A game designer also plays many hours of games created by rival companies. He or she studies a game and, with experience, can break down the good and bad parts of the game in amazing detail.

Game designers who prove their expertise and create great games may rise to the role of lead designer.

Game designers play games made by other companies to learn how they work.

You might call a lead designer the head coach of a project. He or she gathers with a small group of game designers to make basic but important decisions. What kind of a game do we want to create? Where does it take place? Who are the main characters? How will the game compare to other games on the market?

Next, the lead designer sketches out the game's story, or how the game will be played. All of the ideas go into what's called a **game design document** (GDD), an extremely detailed blueprint of how the game will be built.

Game designers need to keep track of a lot of information.

GDDs vary from company to company and game to game. But usually the GDD includes a clear statement on what the game is about, details on the story and characters and world, art notes on everything from colors to sound effects, and the game world's laws of movement. A GDD also details game mechanics, or the way a person will play. Mechanics might include how to move game pieces, shoot an arrow with a bow, or jump over a flaming pit, and the ways players take turns.

The team uses the GDD as a guide when building

the game. As the process goes on, the lead designer keeps the GDD up to date with changes.

The producer, who works with the lead designer, oversees the day-to-day operation of a project, including the schedule and the **budget**.

A game producer manages the lead designer, and recruits a team of talented people to work on the new game. Computer programmers write a game's code. Artists invent the characters, settings, and other visual

THINK ABOUT ART

In the early days, technology forced video game artists to keep their game art blocky and basic. Today, the breathtaking art featured in games finds its way onto the walls of art museums. Tools like digital video and motion capture technology have pushed the art and animation found in video games close to that used to make movies. We may one day consider game creation an art form. If so, video game designers will become as famous as movie directors and musicians.

Creating a video game character takes patience and close attention to detail.

details. Animators make images move. Sound designers drop in the noises, while composers write the music.

Level designers, in the meantime, come up with the details for each of the game's levels of play. One level designer is in charge of a game's artistic elements. Another makes sure the game plays correctly. All the time, the lead designer and level designers work together to ensure each level fits in with the story. The producer, meanwhile, makes sure that the entire game development team, and all the departments, work together in the smoothest way possible.

The lead designer's many responsibilities guarantee a busy workday. He or she has to know when to push the team in one direction, and when to let the team members unleash their own creativity. To rise to the top of the profession, a person needs training and talent, and to put in countless hours of hard work.

CHAPTER 3

EDUCATION

It's never too soon to start building your skills for a career in video games. One easy and fun way: Play games! But do it in a new way. Play like a developer.

Pause the game every so often and think in creative ways about what's going on. Could a different style of music improve a scene? Is the level you're playing too easy, too fast, or too boring? What would you do to make the heroine look cooler? Can you invent three ways to make the dungeon scarier?

Video game designers ask these kinds of questions

every day. Then, they go about finding answers.

Education and training provide a foundation for a career. Some organizations offer courses in programming for kids. Most high schools provide classes in computer programming languages.

Pay close attention to video games, and you can learn a lot about how they work.

Computer skills are very important for a game designer.

A background in painting and drawing gives a developer the visual skills to get ideas across to the design team. Other kinds of art offer valuable training, too. Learning a musical instrument sparks ideas about how to use sound to create mood. Joining the school band is a great way to learn teamwork. Architecture helps a person imagine buildings. **Engineering** does the same for inventing futuristic machinery within the video game, changing the gravity of the game environment, or working on the collision of objects in the game.

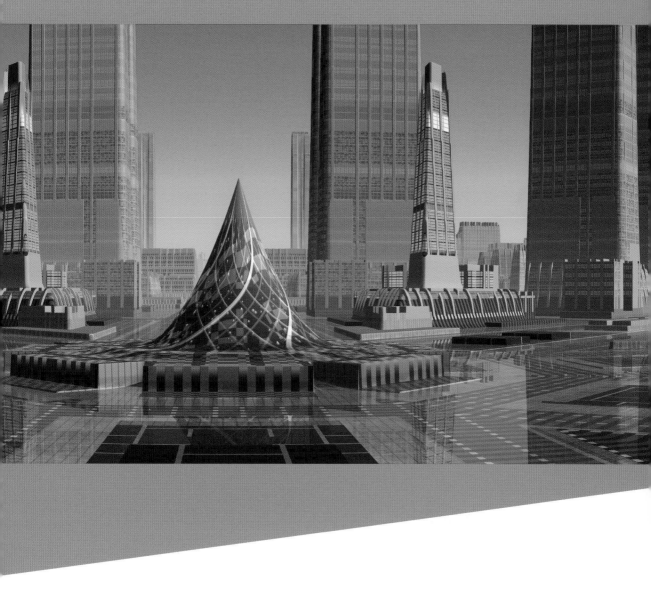

Artists design the settings used in video games.

For this scene to exist, someone needed to design every aspect including the character's face, outfit, and weapon.

Would-be designers usually attend college. Some take classes in computer science or computer engineering. Others may study art. Today, many universities offer a four-year degree in video game design, which includes courses in math, science, technology, and computer science, which teaches how to write software. A growing number of **technical schools** focus on training students for jobs in the gaming industry.

THINK ABOUT SCIENCE

Every fan knows that a game, no matter how unreal, must make sense. Science helps you understand how different systems fit together. That way, you can make a video game universe that, like our real universe, follows a set of rules. Physics, for example, teaches us the laws of movement. Biology, the science of life, offers insight into how to build video life-forms. Even artists need science. Anatomy, for example, trains a person to understand how bodies work and move in logical ways.

CHAPTER 4

TRAINING

Students in search of extra training skip summer break. Instead, they take an **internship** at a game company. These paid or unpaid positions let them work with professionals and get on-the-job experience. An intern who impresses the company may end up with a job at that company after graduation.

Testing games can open doors to a career. Companies give game testers the fancy name of quality assurance (QA) testers. These testers are crucial members of a

Playing an instrument may improve your memory and learning ability. These skills are useful as a game designer.

video game team. The QA staff takes a crack at a game's early versions to find "bugs," or mistakes.

Sounds fun, right? It can be. But you have to enjoy playing the same level of a game over and over and over. A game tester thinks of every possible way of playing through a level. Repeated play is the only way to find all of a game's bugs. For that reason, the best QA team members have a gift for paying attention to tiny details.

Game designers must be comfortable with computers and technology.

Not everyone starts in QA. Other common first jobs include sound technician, programmer, and artist. Hard work, creativity, and leadership skills open doors to being a level designer. From there, a person can rise to producer or lead designer.

Whatever ideas the lead designer proposes must fit in with the schedule and budget mapped out by the project's producer. That means even the most mind-blowing game must fit the plan. Otherwise, the game may be late to stores or cost so much the company developing or publishing the game cannot make a profit from it.

Experience teaches a designer how to make such judgments. By going through the game creation process several times, a person learns what others can (and cannot) do. Being able to carry a project from the idea stage to the final product separates the best game designers from everyone else.

THINK ABOUT ENGINEERING

More and more of today's games let players experiment with their own ideas. If a game you own comes with such tools, check them out! Design a dream house for your virtual characters. Plan out a new racecourse or build an airplane that runs on steam. Tinkering with a game lets you make the same choices and decisions made by video game developers every day. Some people post their "mods," or **modifications**, online. Building a Web site to show off your mods can even help you get the attention of game companies.

CHAPTER 5

THE NEXT LEVEL

Video game designers think beyond consoles and computers. Today, many gaming companies look for chances to become partners with moviemakers.

This partnership may happen in two ways. First, Hollywood sometimes turns a hit video game into a movie. That happened in 2010 with *Prince of Persia*. Second, a video game may become so popular that the company starts creating other products. The game *Angry Birds* inspired everything from shirts and hats to soft drinks, plush dolls, and amusement parks. Sony Pictures

Oculus is a new system for virtual reality games.

even plans to release an *Angry Birds* film.

Video games have already changed in unpredictable ways. In the 1970s, no one could have predicted *Pong* would lead to massively multiplayer online role-playing games (MMORPGs) involving millions of players. Even 20 years ago, designers had no idea the future would be filled with smartphone games like *Clash of Clans*.

A designer has to be ready for the newest technology. New, powerful computers and phones allow companies to create products with more realistic images and faster game play.

*These controllers are shaped like steering wheels,
which makes them perfect for a driving game.*

Other hardware inventions take games in entirely new
directions. Sensors on a tablet or on another device allow
us to play games through body movements. The Nintendo
Wii **pioneered** this kind of play.

But the Wii is just the beginning. A technology
called virtual reality could allow us to "live" inside a
video game. Machinery worn on our bodies, or even
implanted inside our brains, will let us experience a
game with all five senses and real-time movements.

Video games are here to stay. Today gamers spend more time, and money, on games than ever before. Many started gaming as kids with console classics like *Guitar Hero*. Others discovered *FarmVille* and other games on Facebook as adults. In time, today's players will grow up. New waves of fans will continue to join the fun. Exciting careers in video games await designers in the years to come.

THINK ABOUT MATH

Video game creators use geometry, the study of shapes, to make the simplest images look realistic. Take a room in a fantasy game. A large throne seems to sit in front of us. A spectacular chamber stretches away behind the throne. A tiny doorway glows in the distance. The image created by the art team is flat. Geometry equations allow the art team to use lines, shapes, and other elements to trick the human eye into thinking the room looks deep, like in real life.

THINK ABOUT IT

Spend some time playing your favorite video game. Write down what you think the strengths and weaknesses are in its design. Ask a friend or family member to do the same thing. How do your opinions compare? Then go online to look up other reviews that the game received. How much do you agree or disagree with the critics? Defend your views.

Think about some of your favorite books and movies. Are there any that you think could become great video games? Pick one and write down some ideas. How would the player earn points or pass to new levels? Which parts of the story would you make more exciting? What would the characters and setting look like?

LEARN MORE

FURTHER READING

Firestone, Mary. *Nintendo: The Company and Its Founders.* Edina, MN: ABDO, 2011.

Harbour, Jonathan S. *Video Game Programming for Kids.* Independence, KY: Cengage Learning, 2014.

Kaplan, Arie. *The Crazy Careers of Video Game Designers.* New York: Lerner, 2013.

Powell, Marie. *Asking Questions About Video Games.* Ann Arbor, MI: Cherry Lake Publishing, 2016.

WEB SITES

A Digital Dreamer: How to Become a Video Game Programmer
www.adigitaldreamer.com/articles/become-a-game-programmer.htm
Learn about the job outlook as well as the traits and training needed for someone to become a successful video game designer.

Mason Game & Technology Academy
http://potomacacademy.gmu.edu/Classes/GameDesign.html
Do you live near Fairfax, Virginia? Check out some game design classes you can sign up for.

University of Southern California: USC Games
http://games.usc.edu
Browse through this site devoted to one of the top game design programs in the United States.

GLOSSARY

arcades (ar-KAYDZ) rooms or businesses where people pay to play games

budget (BUHJ-it) a plan mapping out how money will be spent on a project

engineering (en-jeh-NEER-ing) the branch of science dedicated to designing and building machines and structures

franchise (FRAN-chize) a group of related games, or one game and its sequels

game design document (GAME dih-ZINE DOK-yuh-muhnt) a written plan that lays out a game's characters, obstacles, goals, and other details

glitches (GLICH-iz) sudden things that go wrong or cause a problem, usually with machinery

internship (IN-turn-ship) a short-term job with a company that is set aside for students, who learn new skills on the job

modifications (mah-duh-fi-KAY-shuhnz) changes made to something; video gamers often shorten the word to "mod"

pioneered (pye-uh-NEERD) was the first or one of the first to attempt a feat

technical schools (TEK-nuh-kuhl SKOOLZ) special kinds of colleges that train students for jobs in certain industries

INDEX

[21ST CENTURY SKILLS LIBRARY]